I0841089

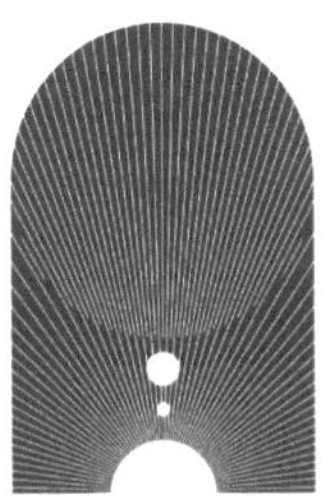

SOLUM JOURNAL

VOLUME III

SOLUM JOURNAL
VOLUME III

AN IMPRINT OF SOLUM LITERARY PRESS

Solum Journal is a biannual literary journal. It is a project of Solum Literary Press, a Christian small press publishing poetry, fiction, homilies, and visual art.

Masthead

Riley Bounds, Publisher and Editor in Chief
Christine Pelliccio, Managing Editor
Douglas J. Lindquist, Content Editor and Theology Editor
Matthew J. Andrews, Poetry Editor
Ryan Rickrode, Fiction Editor
Sarah Christolini, Graphic Designer

SOLUM LITERARY PRESS

2055 E Hampton Ave, 235

Mesa, AZ 85204

(480) 371-9053
info@solumpress.com

For submission guidelines, purchasing, and subscription information, please visit https://www.solumpress.com.

CONTENTS

To the abused

. . . the downward Way of despair
is not yet the way out . . . — Stephen Mitchell, "Kafka"

CALL TO PRAYER

Lory Widmer Hess

Annunciation

Don't try to understand
                        a mystery

Just listen
            and wait
                    for no answer

Listen to what nature
                    left unsaid

The gap
        between seed
                    and tree

Listen like Mary
                trembling
                        alone

Overborne
        by urgent creation

Asking only How?
                and answering

Yes

Lory Widmer Hess has been an editor, graphic designer, and English teacher, but her most transformative experience has come through her past decade of working with adults with developmental disabilities. Her writing has been published in *Parabola*, *Kosmos Quarterly*, *Ruminate*, *Braided Way*, *Untold Volumes*, and other print and on-line publications. She blogs about life, language, and literature at enterenchanted.com.

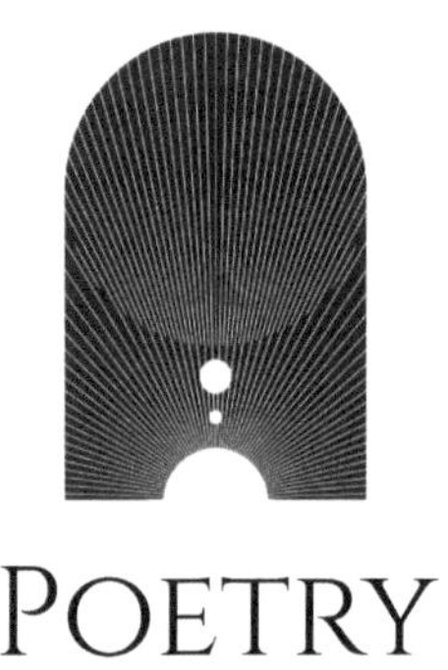

POETRY

CAROLINE LIBERATORE

Dawn After a Summer Storm

The morning hums yellow after the romp
of the night's thunderstorms, treetops heaving
to catch their breath.

The morning hums yellow, and my soul
is weathered by yet another static sight
indeterminate.

The morning hums yellow. It's sickening
how the sun so pathetically insists upon
itself.

The morning hums yellow, and I turn over
to slumber, rumbling with hunger
for a clearer dawn.

Caroline Liberatore is a poet and librarian from Cleveland, Ohio. Her poetry has appeared in a variety of publications, including *Ekstasis*, *Agape Review*, and *Amethyst Review*. Caroline recently joined staff at *LogoSophia Magazine*, where she is a regular contributor. Much of her current work might be described as taut between transcendent utterances of the gospel and everyday grit. You can read more at carolinelib.wordpress.com.

EMILY NEUHARTH

Soak

Full moon in dark contrast.
        Sitting close, feeling
Far. The hot tub holds us.

Steam rises, tears drop.
        His words float on water:
Leave me wanting.

Something fell tonight.
        I need more than him but
Won't the break drown me.

I look up, down:
        White sphere against navy.
God help me

Do it. Snow cloaks my shoulders
        Burning wet skin I let it
Stay and grow colder.

I still want for him:
        Soothe my pain, fill me.
But I'm on my own

Sinking into night.
        Won't the grief lift from my arms—
Rise, chlorine incense.

Is that you God
        Moon shining down at me blurry,
Ghostly reflection.

Emily Neuharth currently writes from Chicago, one of her many home-places. She is pursuing an MFA at Northwestern Ulnivery. Her work has appeared at Salon, Petrichor, and DASH. https://emilyneuharth.wordpress.com/ @emerinn

Kristina Erny

Horeb, Mountain of the Lord

1 Kings 19, an acrostic and almost contrapuntal

How many times can we pass by?

Open years Elijah   into the day before the crows, your own
red creek bottom. Dry-stone   fears that you can't hear us.

Elijah wait with your
back to the hurricane. We are

moved to what burns you.

O, get your head out from
under the rock

note small   seismic differences in
temperature   the hair on your arms standing up
again like it did the last time.

Isn't there always a last time?

Note the way the air stills and the

        ravens become contemplative

what they question.
How they know us.

Elijah   They have
reached into their   tiny minds and have bowed down already,
ever dark   even on this forsaken and holy

transom.

Here we are. Why are we still here?

Eat this whisper, a wafer of our kindness.

Lean your lobe over and place it
on the ground.

                      It is best to
reach back into the vacuum and shut off your own
devices, black them out until you are

melted down, tucked in,
eager, ready to be threaded out,

taken once again into our palms. Who better than

Elijah to be consoled here and now;

                              he runs away and whines,
lists all the ways we've failed him,
inches closer and closer   to the edge of the cliff,
just cloak,   just feathers, just

a miniscule
human ear.

Kristina Erny is a third-culture poet who grew up in South Korea and elsewhere abroad. She holds an MFA from the University of Arizona. Her work has been the recipient of the Tupelo Quarterly Inaugural Poetry Prize and the Ruskin Art Club Poetry Award, as well as a finalist for the Coniston Prize. Her poems have appeared in *The Los Angeles Review*, *Yemassee*, *Blackbird*, and *Tupelo Quarterly*, among other journals. She currently lives and works in Shanghai, China, where she teaches at an international school with her partner and their three young children. Her first book of poetry, *Elijah Fed by Ravens*, is forthcoming in 2024 from Solum Literary Press.

Louie Land

Too Tired For Anger, I Have Become Obsessed

With the trappings
of what we'll call progress: chutes
splitting sidewalks into high-rises
of concrete and metal and glass
in a motion towards transparency

With the names of particles
I save for poems—*photons*
bear light   *gluons* carry force *fermions*
are particles of matter—but whose
function I fail to comprehend
beyond the definition

With fatigue as the privilege
of those who have given up the fight
or had it kicked from them

With sublimation

With the smell of sulfur

With an interview with Jim Hall
saying *I feel like Miles*
could play silence better
than some guys could play
notes

With transmissions beamed forty-three

million miles between Earth
and *Curiosity*, the twenty-minute absence
before the rover's response

With bottling our sun in green glass—
what my grandmother calls *Depression
ware*—and pawning jade lanterns
for a dollar and a quarter to anyone
who asks for a light

With who owns the water particles
crystalizing from our breath
after they leave our vision to be
inhaled by another

With how energy that spins
atoms into suns marks lovers
as shadowed phantoms on brick

With gestures towards leaving:
the lacing of boots, the clearing
of throats

With the light pollution that backscatters
across the atmosphere
into translucence, cities burning, obscuring
nebulae

With the rusted shopping cart
covered in a blue tarp down
the street, how it seems, in the rain,
a man in a slicker of sapphires
bending across a stroller
to brush his daughter's soaked hair

Louie Land is a poet, novelist, and modern jazz musician living in central Pennsylvania. He holds an MFA in creative writing from the University of Idaho. His poems have previously appeared in *Heron Tree*, *Martin Lake Journal*, *Poetica Review*, *FRiGG*, and elsewhere. His pop-rock album, *Afterglow*, was released in 2018.

Birdie Marie Rodriguez

Grace Changes Us and Change is Painful

*"All human nature vigorously resists grace because grace changes us and
the change is painful." —Flannery O'Connor*

you forget who
you are in
the attic

as you recover
a poppy
pressed in a wrinkle
in time

the blush stained
paper approaches
as a reflection
of yet another
bygone self
and you face
your brevity,
shake its hand
and say hello

you've been many
a thing
perched on the hem
of a dusky ocean
within
seasons that soften
into one another
unhurried
and deliberate

as how the colors

bleed in one
breath with t
he turning

of a kaleidoscope

your faults peel
like sunburnt
skin and
worthy
aspirations fatten
over a dozen
infinities
to unmask
a yearning
for the holy
sting

you dwell
in the fever
of every conversion
on the shore
of a mammoth sea
that is undeterred
by the changing
of the guard
unbothered
by the glorious
ache
in the twang
of all your
goodbyes

Birdie Marie Rodriguez is an accomplished folk artist and an emerging poet. She has a passion for storytelling, and is inspired by history, theology, nature and family. She is an alumna of The American Musical and Dramatic Academy New York City, and currently lives on the Coastal Plains of North Carolina with her husband and three children.

JOSHUA GAGE

The Call

Last night, I dreamt
God falling
as maple leaves.
I awoke to find
my porch dyed
red with Autumn.

A cold wind crawls
down from the mountain
to wail my porch clean.
Do not let the wind
mourn here. Tonight,
I sleep with my window
open, my door unlocked.

Joshua Gage is an ornery curmudgeon from Cleveland. His newest chapbook, *blips on a screen,* is available on Cuttlefish Books. He is a graduate of the Low Residency MFA Program in Creative Writing at Naropa University. He has a penchant for Pendleton shirts, Ethiopian coffee, and any poem strong enough to yank the breath out of his lungs. IG: @pottygok

JEFF HARDIN

The Text We Read Is Just The One We See

How to say a thing and then to hear its implications
requires more years than we are given. I still dwell
on an oak in a field no longer there, replaced by
three houses whose stories are not my own. I trim
climbing roses obtained from cuttings of cuttings
first planted by my great-grandmother born in 1894.
She used to hide my brother in the folds of her dress.
She outlived her husband by a generation. Inheritance
that should have come down his line went down another
instead. My brother once wandered away, was found
hours later on a rock above the river. He would have
drowned had he slipped. No one knows if he almost did.
He was three, an age in which all our futures struggle
for supremacy. The text we read is just the one we see,
not all the versions that might have been. The barn loft
I sat in as a child is no longer there, but I can still feel
the rungs of its ladder against the arches of my feet.
Is that why I try to find a higher vantage point from
which to look upon my life? Off in the distance, corn
tassels hold a secret whose whispers I lean toward.
They sound like a river hidden in fog across which
a voice is summoning all who will come. Daily I
disappear from my life, sometimes only a moment,
sometimes for hours. What if it turns out we've all
been disinherited from a future we cannot imagine?
I have no idea what's indeterminate or irrefutable.
The wind covers as much as it uncovers and vice versa.
A word says more than it says even if no one hears.

Belief is a metaphor for doubt, doubt a metaphor for
how we move all our lives toward beliefs we can bear.

Jeff Hardin is the author of seven collections of poetry, most recently *Watermark, A Clearing Space in the Middle of Being*, and *No Other Kind of World*. His books have been honored with the Nicholas Roerich Prize, the Donald Justice Prize, and the X. J. Kennedy Prize. Recent and forthcoming poems appear in *The Southern Review, Hudson Review, Poetry Northwest, The Laurel Review, Southern Poetry Review,* and elsewhere. He lives and teaches in TN. Visit his website: jeffhardin.weebly.com.

CLAUDIA STANEK

Birches

See, against the light? The body's
landscape is marked by pain's highway.
Fracture lies within. The glowing
Sea of the mind-stream twists itself
into noir nano-second glass.
God plants you beneath birches.
Angels rattle the leaves in chant.

Claudia Stanek's work has been turned into a libretto, been part of an art exhibition, and been translated into Polish. Her poems exist online, in print, and in her chapbook *Language You Refuse to Learn*. She holds an MFA from Bennington College. Her rescued dogs try to manage her life.

MATTEA GERNENTZ

Pilgrim

Palms pressed, swept
up in sea breezes
and silent epiphanies,
this revelation born of
whispered breath and
surging tide, roaring near
while I could not gather
fickle courage to jump,
a rippled boulder slick
beneath shifting feet.
Cockle, spoon clam,
rayed artemis, limpet
clutched tightly, stowed
in skeletal harvest.
The boy among ruins
skipping stones, one,
two, that hover glibly,
suspended in delight,
before sinking still.
I pray that he will not
watch me fall and leap.

Mattea Gernentz is a poet and art curator from Tennessee based in Edinburgh, Scotland. With studies in art history, literature, and psychology, she is an alumna of St Andrews and Wheaton College. Selected as one of Scotland's 2022 Next Generation Young Makars, her writing meditates on themes of beauty, memory, and faith. Her work has been featured in *Kodon*, *The Pub*, *ST.ART Magazine*, and various anthologies.

EDEN THEULE

Blessed are the Poor

"[Love is] tough and shriveled and shoeless and homeless,
always lying in the dirt without a bed, sleeping at people's doorsteps
and in roadsides under the sky"
-Plato, *The Symposium*

When I see that sycamore tree,
Leafless under the blazing sky,
It's only an image, the impression of light
Against the retina, flipped and shuffled
From eye to mind. If I were to hold
The tree in my arms or even be held
In its branches, would I possess it even then?
Maybe partly, for the space of a minute,
Before it's scooped up into the unwitnessable.
The gift is always larger the hands I reach
To take it with – it pours between my fingers
And I'm left panting in the sand.
The needing never stops, however
Much light is poured down on us,
Drowsing over petitionary prayers,
Unsatisfied with comfort,
Holding on for Dear Life
          (Because, God knows, it is dear)
To our craving for bread, tomorrow as today,
And for something better than what we want now.

Eden Theule is a cook, flower grower, and emerging poet living on the Central Coast of California. She is a recent graduate of Biola University, where she worked as editor-in-chief of *Inkslinger* literary journal. Her poetry pulls together her broad interests in literature, agriculture, spiritual formation, and food.

JONATHAN CHAN

prayer (xvii)

assuming a bedside manner,

    body supine, back aching, midnight shade

      taut across

the ceiling, the walls, the lines echo –

    'far from the kingdom, how steady

      is the room.'

    steady for a dream, the lush ferment

        of green, walking along

      the tangle of orchards, walking

       with a three-mile-an-hour

       god,

    listening, plodding, bearing all

the weight,

     and all the grief,

    of an oxygen sapped. night speech

is like a still

     performance. he unfurls a hand, points

to the four corners veiled in mist,

      the blue sky spreading over a thousand

           lengths, the sundial waiting as the bones

              of a chapel. a monastic sits,

      aflame in black ecstasy, sharpening

and seething, counting the interruptions

          of a burning

                    bush.

in the garden, the grass is fine as floss,

          the grass is blue as jade.

Jonathan Chan is a writer and editor of poems and essays. Born in New York to a Malaysian father and South Korean mother, he was raised in Singapore and educated at Cambridge and Yale Universities. He is the author of the poetry collection *going home* (Landmark, 2022) and Managing Editor of poetry.sg. He has recently been moved by the work of Jason Wee, G. C. Waldrep, and Pádraig Ó Tuama. He has an abiding interest in faith, identity, and creative expression. More of his writing can be found at jonbcy.wordpress.com..

WHITNEY RIO-ROSS

Saint Agnes, Fallen Near Baptismal

Urakami Cathedral, Nagasaki

There was so much she couldn't have
imagined. That the knuckles kneading her
to life would one day gnarl to stone.

How the pool would soon thirst
to baptize even talons splashing through
the sacred. Why howls would lace
the silence she must learn to love.

That her dreams of breath would choke
to nightmare as vapor dissolved
each echo she believed. Whether her god
was named false or true.

But surely she learned what I haven't kept
still enough to prove—that even the holiest waters
won't reflect all they drink in.

It's still a matter of lighting.

Whitney Rio-Ross is author of the chapbook *Birthmarks* (Wipf & Stock) and poetry editor for *Fare Forward.* Her poetry has appeared in *Presence Journal, Psaltery & Lyre, Relief Journal, America Magazine,* and elsewhere. She was the winner of the 2021 Sacred Poetry Contest and lives in Nashville, TN, with her husband and pups.

Elizabeth Bates

Visions of Christmas Eve

A curl of smoke
      rises from
a rooftop &
the distinctive
scent overwhelms the vaporous
winter air.
Relatives share a meal,
the heat of a wood fireplace warming
their backs.

Smoke & snow
illustrate the landscape
      on a brief drive.

Church
windows hum with harmonious carols
sung by
three-part choirs,
      faces illuminated
      under orange candlelight.
        The midnight
      hour gleams.
Jesus is
placed in the manger.
An altar boy
puts out the candle
        & the smoke curls
in the sanctuary
at the end of Mass.

The lights
go out.
Families head
home. The outside
world is snow
& shadows. A father
throws
logs on the fire
          & the smoke billows.
Children pull covers to their chins &
struggle to keep their eyes closed.
For the night,
invisible and visible
          trade places.

Elizabeth Bates is a Best of the Net and Pushcart-nominated writer living in Washington state with her family. She is the author of poetry chapbooks, *Mosaics & Mirages* (Fahmidan Publishing & Co., 2022) and *Rose Gold: Betty White Poems* (The Daily Drunk, 2023). Follow her on Twitter and Instagram @ElizabethKBates.

MICHAEL J. ORTIZ

Dust and Light

Come with me,

we're going further into
this witness,

this action that is and isn't itself,
that creaks open

the door of time.

Once when a boy

I opened a tall cabinet
in our cellar:

it looked like a coffin standing
straight up,
with simple lines,

its door swung open as the morning
washed through windows near the ceiling

where tangles of pipes hung.

At once, dust exhaled from
fifty mason jars,
stilled in their embossed

and orderly rows.

I felt like a priest bringing one out,

holding it to the light,
its tiny sky now full

of sun.

Michael J. Ortiz lives in Maryland and teaches writing. He is the author of two
books. He and his wife have four children, all better educated than he is.

CAMERON BROOKS

The Seagull Scans a Fallow Field

The seagull scans
a fallow field
in search of God

knows what.
Have you lost your way,
mistaking this God

forsaken wilderness
for the shores you were
created for?

Perhaps you were gulled
by the Prairie
waves into believing

that you had discovered
country good for more
than flying over—

maybe even a place
to stay; it's okay,
so did we.

Cameron Brooks is an M.F.A. candidate at Seattle Pacific University. He holds an M.A. from Princeton Seminary and serves as Managing Editor for <u>Vanora</u>, an artist collaboration website. His poems have appeared in *Poetry East*, *North Dakota Quarterly*, *Ekstatis Magazine*, *Ad Fontes*, and elsewhere. <u>Cameron</u> lives in Sioux Falls, South Dakota.

PATRICK T. REARDON

Adman walked south

Adman walked south on Leviathan Boulevard
toward Brooklyn,
announcing:

> *I will anthem sing tomorrow, prophet talk.*
> *I will speak in tongues.*
>
> *I will page poems, climb tree, sweep dirt,*
> *change rules.*
>
> *Draw the map,*
> *find the Savior, publish diligent voices.*
> *Hearken to the sound, scratch the itch.*

It was Manhattan so no one paid him mind.

He wore camo sweatpants
below a sharp white shirt
with a blue-pattern tie from his fraternity.

He dragged behind him on a leash
a black and white stuffed puppy, not large.

> *Rise up, set down, push away,*
> *elbow, head-butt, go, come, go,*
> *let my skin find the secret commandments.*
>
> *I will oath. I will shut. I will vex.*
>
> *Tomorrow, not today.*

He stopped in the McDonald's
near Avenue of the Saints
and took his Egg McMuffin up to the second floor,
empty except for a Bible study group.

He was sure they were praying for his soul.

He went over
and whispered into the ear of the young pastor,
fresh from his riverside jog:

> *I will bring frogs to the altar*
> *and unguents, oils from Arabia,*
> *first-born live stock*
> *for the gleaming blade.*

> *Interview the lost tribes.*
> *Survey the communion of saints.*
> *Answer aboriginal questions.*
> *Submit to interrogatories.*

> *Touch brass. Touch gold. Touch water-worn wood.*

> *I will open my mouth tomorrow to the rain.*

The paster continued without missing a beat,
"Turn your prayer books to Chapter 13."

And Adman left his table unbussed.

On the sidewalk outside, he opened his arms wide
— forcing several tourists from Chagrin Falls
to step into the street,
scrunching noses as if he smelled (he didn't)
and already composing texts back home —
and sang out:

> *Fire the newspaper. Fire the straw.*
> *Fire my infant photos.*

> *Walk the sidewalks bellowing, free or mad.*

> *Grope. Grasp. Grip.*

I will plant the sunflower.
Crush the rotten peach under my heel.
Spill the rotten milk on soil.
Step past the nest-fallen egg.
Intoxicate on grass mown aroma.

On that short Dutch street, Numbers Avenue,
Adman refused to look up
at the shrine towering over him
and all the other small beings
skittering the concrete lanes.
No romantic, he.

He was in the subway that day
and came up to the rain of bodies.

He has stored in his closet
all the clothes he wore that day.
still covered with gray dust.

He almost wore the outfit this day,

I will proverb tomorrow, psalm a lamentation.
I will flee down Chronicles Road.
Sightsee Transfiguration
Circle the Black Stone.
Dine on the Mount.
Leave a footprint
on my brother's bloody backyard sidewalk.

Tomorrow I will roll the stone away.

Answer the bell.
Answer the phone.
Answer what is not asked.

Fire the wood idol.

I will tell the story of my life.
At the Bridge, he turns back.

He will not cross water.
He takes out his cellphone
and calls his dead mother.

I will fence land.
Carve soil.
Follow lines to their end.

Fire the evidence.

Observe the proprieties.
Provide the necessities.

Tomorrow I will be human.

My foot will step in the right direction.

She picks up as he finishes the message.

She tells him to straighten up
and fly right.

She tells him to hold that tiger.

Patrick T. Reardon, a three-time Pushcart Prize nominee, has authored ten books, including the poetry collections *Requiem for David* (Silver Birch), *Darkness on the Face of the Deep* (Kelsay) and *The Lost Tribes* (Grey Book). Forthcoming is his memoir in prose poems *Puddin': The Autobiography of a Baby* (Third World). His website is patricktreardon.com.

Ben Egerton

Unknowing

you can't see the summit
from the carpark for cloud

but when you reach it
you're accepted

into the weather   as into
a place a child might choose

        somewhere to see from
but not be seen in

        & you take it all in—
the white car

on Wilton Road
        its headlights reflecting

in the wet tarmac
        pitch markings

on the park   flank
of suburb laid out opposite

like a butcher's chart—
        you run yourself

to the edge
of exhaustion on your assault

on the hill   six times
since last December

via this route   up & back
& what for?   your father

once asked, *what are you
running from?*   he never asks,

*who are you
running towards?*   you don't seek

or expect anything
except to catch something

of his silence   to run downhill
through the pines

Ben Egerton is the author of *The Seed Drill* (Kelsay). His poetry has been widely published in print and online journals. Ben lives in Wellington, New Zealand, where he teaches in the Faculty of Education at Te Herenga Waka | Victoria University of Wellington.

VERONICA MCDONALD

little one

a small boy's head
       soaked in blood
is he my son
       or the son of my enemy
either way I am
       created to love
the way a mother should
       after the birth pains
when life emerges from
       blood sweat feces
a crocus grows
       under ice and snow
then dies in four years
       in a stranger's arms
cracked concrete chunks cover
       soft spring grass

Veronica McDonald is a fiction writer, poet, visual artist, and founding editor of *Heart of Flesh Literary Journal*. She is a former atheist turned Christian, and thanks Jesus everyday for turning her world upside down. Visit her at veronicamcdonald.com.

RUSSELL ROWLAND

Not Looking for Angels

A pair of herons passed over earlier,
the union two make. You've seen how stilted
they walk, mirroring their reflections

as they stalk shallows for fish—
well, I can report that overhead they appear
as aerodynamic as the Concorde.

I don't look for angels as such.
That's testing. I want to see what's up there,
when other heads are bowed.

Perfectly fine people keep vigils
in a way that suggests our bluebirds, hawks,
ospreys aren't heavenly enough.

These good folk haven't realized
the psaltery that goes on at cloud level,
or matched feathers to the rainbow.

They expect a Host, and I hope
they get one. Two herons did for me today:
their flightpath was their praise.

Seven-time Pushcart Prize nominee **Russell Rowland** writes from New Hampshire's Lakes Region, where he has judged high-school Poetry Out Loud competitions. His work appears in *Except for Love: New England Poets Inspired by Donald Hall* (Encircle Publications), and "*Covid Spring, Vol. 2*" (Hobblebush Books). His latest poetry book, *Wooden Nutmegs*, is available from Encircle Publications.

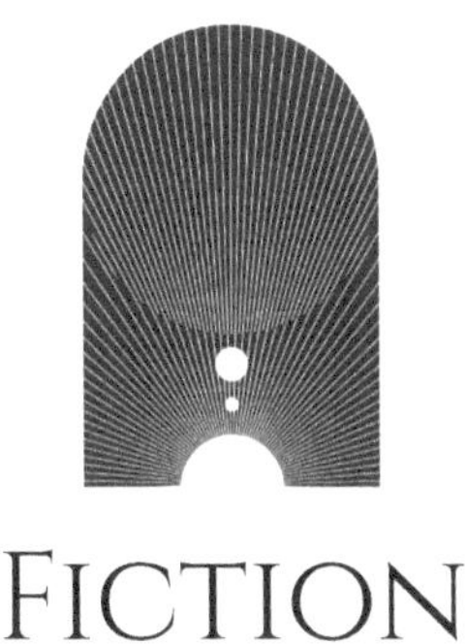

FICTION

Shannon Baker

The Sycamore

For what will it profit a man if he gains the whole world, and loses his own soul?
~ Mark 8:36

Out beyond the sycamore tree is where the men would go to lose their souls. There was no specific place, no marking—not even an upturned clod of grass along the banks of the river or a fossilized boot print in the deep, red clay—nothing, nothing at all that would give a passing sojourner pause, that would make them think, *here, here is where it happened. Here is where the men beat the odds and lost it all.*

Like the earth, the river is quiet. The sycamore, too. It stands tall and old, mottled bark peeling in places, leaves broad and canopied, casting shade on the river grasses. The wind passes through the green, *whooshing*, but the tree stays silent. What happened is done; what more can be said? Volition is a terrible, beautiful thing.

Once or twice, a man was on his way to out beyond the sycamore but stopped. Instead, he climbed the sycamore to see better. His feet scraped the red-and-white bark of the sycamore, which hoisted him up to the highest branches. The leaves danced in soft breezes that day, joining the chatter of passing crowds. Branches were broken in the man's hasty descent, but the sycamore only felt the promise of renewal. Those days were good, when it was climbed, when its branches shed both bark and wisdom and it was more than just a monument to things of old. When it was climbed for truth and not passed for profit.

As time went by, however, fewer and fewer stopped to climb the sycamore. Their hands would graze its peeling trunk, brushing the red-and-white wood with wistful fingers, almost as if their souls knew what they were about to do before they did. Which, in most cases, was quite true—and the sycamore always felt a tremor through its trunk, passed along by their touch: the internal war of the soul versus the man. But volition is a terrible, beautiful thing, and it is Man's, not Nature's, to decide what to do with.

***

It started with a hunger, or rather, an absence. An absence of satisfaction. If a man wasn't satisfied, he was hungry, and though he might pretend otherwise, his chief priority in life was quelling that hunger. The hunger would come. Without fail it would come—what he had was not enough, though it was never supposed to be. But instead of treating his hunger as proof of this fact, the man treated it like a beast—and a beast it would become. It would grow, slowly, steadily, until it consumed the man's thoughts with its gaping, vacant expression: *Feed me*. And so, he would look for ways to feed this "appetite"—to quiet it—to make room for other appetites. Because that was the thing about feeding appetites: when one was dethroned, another inevitably took its place. It might be of a different sort, with a different voice, a different drive, with a different recipe for satiation. But whatever the appetite was, there was one consistent truth about the *next* appetite in line: It was always bigger.

He would build for the appetite an empire, thinking he was protecting it, thinking he was reeling it in, making it a home, keeping it happy, so that it wouldn't destroy him. But over time, the appetite lodged itself somewhere he could not see, and it would carve its dwelling slowly, embedding deeper and deeper, making for itself a home in the real estate of his soul.

The hunger was never the problem. The hunger was *good*. But the men took what was good and made it a beast, and the beasts dug holes, and the men tried to fill them. They poured fixes into the yawning, creaturely mouths of their appetites, gorging the beasts but starving themselves.

And as time went by, the sycamore began to notice: The crowds of men that went out beyond it were of a certain way, and the ones that stopped to climb—fewer and farther between, yes, but there was the occasional man— were of another way. All the men looked different, and at first glance, you could not tell one from the other—those who would choose to stop and those who would continue out beyond—but there was something distinct when they brushed by the sycamore's trunk, something internal, something visible to the constant, patient gaze that only Nature could manage. It was difficult to put into words—and Nature did not—but it came down to something of an awareness. An awareness of emptiness. It could be seen in the eyes of the men who stopped: They stumbled over branches and roots until they reached the sycamore, and then they paused, eyes wide and searching, sensitive to the tug within. The emptiness was there in the black wells of their pupils, but it vibrated. It had been found out, and it was being given up. And for those that climbed the sycamore, it was handed over. Having handed over their emptiness, the men would climb back down, eyes shining, and the sycamore would shudder, passing what was handed over down through its trunk, flushing it by its root system, and the water that coursed in the river would swirl and eddy and dissolve it all. Gone. And the men who were once empty would be full, turning back to their life and clasping their souls tight to their chests.

The crowds of men that went out beyond the sycamore felt the tug in their souls the same way, but their yearning fingers grazed the bark of the tree only for a moment before they flung themselves forward and out beyond. Their eyes held the same emptiness as the other men's, but the difference was this: They did not notice they were empty. It could be better said in this way: The men that stopped at the sycamore had a full, dizzying emptiness, and they knew it. The men that went out beyond had a dizzying, empty fullness, and they did not know it. They held loosely to their souls as they jostled past the sycamore, putting themselves up as collateral for the game that lay ahead.

The game that lay ahead. It was a ruthless game—enticing and unforgiving, and the more they played, the more they lost, though it didn't feel like losing in the moment. But the sycamore knew better. Of the men that went out beyond, very few of them came back. There was the occasional man, the man who played the game and saw that he was losing, and, at the last moment, snatched his soul from the creaturely mouths of other men's appetites and hugged it to his chest. Turning on his heel, he struggled to ignore the voices that grasped at him—that tried to pull him back—but something *else* was stronger now, and he pushed past other greedy bodies and flailing souls and ran, ran, *ran* back the way he had come. Sometimes it took a painfully long time—he'd forgotten the way—but the Something Else was resilient, and nose to the wind, feet stumbling and catching, he followed the scent carried on the wind from the old tree by the river. When the sycamore saw him barreling over the hill and along the banks of the river towards it, chest heaving, eyes red and frantic, the sycamore waved its branches, the wind *whooshed* through its gaps, and it bent towards the man, tremors rippling down its trunk, stilling only when the man collapsed at its base and pressed his palm to the bark with the relief of return, his quivering soul quieting within him.

The wind frequently followed the course of the river and over the hill to out beyond, letting its fragrance turn the heads of the many men whose Something Else still quivered, even buried deep within after years of playing the game. The wind would tickle lightly, and some men would respond, but those whose appetites were so engorged often did not glance at the stirring grasses that played at their feet. Instead, they set the sights of their appetites on other men's souls, and there they cast their lots.

The men playing the game did not look different from any other man. They were simply *more*: their edges were often crisper, their mouths often wider, their eyes often sharper. Their voices were louder, fueled by the growling of their appetites, though these stayed hidden as they burrowed deeper, deeper, deeper into the men's souls. The men with larger appetites preyed on the men with smaller appetites, and when a man first went to the out beyond, it took some time for him to learn who to play with. He first played with the men he arrived with, whose appetites were also yet juvenile and untrained. One appetite would surge and lash out, and the other, unsure how to defend itself, would fall injured. Snarling and retreating to its corner, it would take a piece of the man's soul and hand it over. The other man's appetite would feast—nothing tasted quite so good as another man's potential—and it would grow, already looking for the next round.

Looking on the carnage, it was easy to assume that the man whose appetite feasted had won. He became more...*more*, and this was all anyone wanted in the out beyond, never realizing that if *more* was the goal, it couldn't possibly be reached. At the end of the game, there would be no winners, but even in the moment, onlookers would have been mistaken: The men who lay broken and bleeding, having just handed over a piece of their eviscerated soul, still had appetites, and these raged and howled and picked the men up again so that they could throw themselves back into the game, limping, wincing, eyes slanted and dark and bent once again on *more*. Meanwhile, the appetite of the man who had feasted licked its gluttonous lips, buried itself more deeply into the man's soul, held on tighter and, never satisfied for long, craftily set its sights on new arrivals.

The game space was quite a sight. A battleground, any onlooker would say (though, of course, out beyond, there were none, only players). Appetites prowled while souls cowered, doing their best to hide in the open expanse while they nursed their wounds. But a dying soul was vulnerable, and the men would not shield them, not even their own—their eyes were so set on the beasts. And so, when a soul was finished, the potential vanquished, there was nothing left but the husk of the man who realized too late his mistake. And the ground burned in indignation, a smoke signal rising to the sky, but of course, no one paid it any attention.

Fires ravaged the plains, beasts stalked souls, men egged them on. Everything was desolate, but if an onlooker fixed his gaze on the men who were *more*, the ones whose appetites gorged freely, he might have forgotten the charred rocks and blood-streaked dirt. He might have done away with the image of the fallen on the grass, whose souls flitted in desperation over their disillusioned eyes, trying to distract them from their own appetite that growled within, alive and well. For the men who were *more* were captivating, even to the fallen, with their crowns and their winnings draped across their shoulders—shiny, resplendent things that beckoned new arrivals in droves— *this, this is what we're playing for*. An onlooker would be mesmerized too, until the winds blew again from the sycamore, and, guiding their eyes upwards, reminded them that the crowns were smoking, too.

And so it went. The men played, casting their lots in a game they were already bound to lose, consuming one another and being consumed themselves. But though the sycamore sent its wild, knowing wind and rustled the grasses at their feet, the men kept on. They became *more*, even as their buried souls yearned, even as their bleeding faces turned back towards the river and the tree that they had passed. Still the wind blew, sometimes in wisps and sometimes in gusts: In the worst case, it still alleviated Nature from the burning towers of fire that scorched the face of the plains; in the best case, it lifted the eyes and nose of one man among thousands, a man whose weary, beaten soul was still open to the Something Else that churned within him, beckoning him home.

The return—the sycamore was old and tired, but oh, it lived for the return. In the return, after stumbling through the plains and following the wind, the man would tremble against the tree, shaking not so much from the fatigue of his journey but from the good newness of the cool red-and-white bark against his cheek. For as he rested against the solid trunk, the horrors of the game he had played seemed to pass through his mind and into the sycamore, which accepted them, flushing them out through its roots and into the river below. The man did not forget the game itself—it was necessary to remember—but gradually his soul breathed evenly again, no longer tormented by the appetites that had relentlessly sought its life. And when the man became strong enough, as he learned to climb the tree, he found that he did not miss the empty fullness he had left behind.

***

There is much more that could be said about the game, and the men of *more*, and their smoldering crowns. But at the end of it all, what more *should* be said? The same thing that allowed the burning of the plains also allowed the heeding of the wind and the climbing of the tree. Should it not have been so? And if not, what then? A more sinister fate, surely, than volition—that terrible and beautiful thing.

No one can quite say what ended the game once and for all, but like the river, the earth is quiet now. Beasts do not prowl the plains and souls do not cower in fear. New grasses have grown over the ravaged land of before. Clay that was once imprinted with the shapes of fallen men has been smoothed over by many seasons of rain, the stench of the air fumigated by ever-passing gusts. Yes—the only sound out beyond the sycamore is that of the wind, which still whispers and blows, stirring the grasses, taking the few remaining memories of the horror they endured and carrying them back on the breeze, back to the swirling eddies of the river and the cleansing roots of the sycamore, which stands there still, quietly healing, at the gate to the out beyond.

Having grown up along the North Shore of Lake Superior, **Shannon Baker** has always felt most at home in the outdoors. Now, living in central Iowa, she still draws inspiration from the wild spaces around her to create stories and poetry bent on transmitting messages of hope, joy, and redemption that is ever-present in the natural world. When she's not writing, Shannon enjoys reading, kayaking, hiking, traveling, picking away at guitar or fiddle, connecting with people, and dreaming of ways to visit all the national parks. Her other poems and stories appear in *Plain China: National Anthology of the Best Undergraduate Writing* and elsewhere. You can read more of Shannon's stories and poetry on her website: https://shanbake13.wixsite. com/shannon-baker.

Elizabeth Genovise

Van Gogh at Dawn

There must have been a perilous moment, a juncture at which he could have shelved palette and paint prematurely, like a weary traveler at an oasis who submits to tardy comfort until his purpose has faded from memory. He might have chuffed out the candles and tucked the empty chairs beneath the table, as one does with unwelcome questions— or ghosts. Surely the tea-kettle and the cotton called his name, and like softly-falling rain, the murmur of city voices, of crowds, reached him at the blue hour to whisper its hypnotic refrain. Perhaps there was a night in which he stared out the clouded glass at the amber wink of distant life and thought to himself, *no further. I am tired.*

On this night he collapsed onto his battered bunk with a muffled moan. As he passed fitfully into sleep he had the errant thought that the soul inhabited a house not entirely its own. In this house a stern father ruled, and a passionate son was sometimes in, sometimes out, and a little spirit moved like smoke through the halls. It was the spirit-child—who liveliest when the son was away—that Vincent yearned always to catch in his arms. From time to time, he had attained his end, or perhaps the child had caught *him* and held on. In these moments, what was true made itself known in yellow and cobalt blue, and oh, what the canvas spoke . . . but at what cost? It was not just bodily depletion Vincent feared, the sapping of muscle and bone. It was that if he remained so caught, the little spirit on his back would compel him into new rooms, new landscapes too dense and palpitating for the constitution of an ordinary man. The fruit spangling the trees was too rich in its bittersweetness; the air was so charged that it passed over dry fields like a great crackling comb until even the cast-off seeds stirred themselves into cyclones that leaved and budded against all laws of nature. Sometimes, in his weariness and fear, Vincent had let the spirit fall from him even as he set his brush aside. Sometimes he dreamt of weightless flight, and could almost prefer this easy ride to the trials and excursions of a soul on foot.

For him sleep has always proffered a velvet relief, until this night when he finds himself on the twilit shore of a colossal sea. Sand glitters beneath his feet, studded with tiny round stones. Heavy indigo clouds, their bellies refracting the coral blush of the falling sun, are mirrored in the waves so that two worlds seem to envelop a third, a midgard, as the past and future cradle the present between them like a child. Vincent steps closer to the water's edge and peers down. Here is a black opal's trem- bling borealis, waters brimming with occult blue and scarlet and green. He is two men as he

stares into the deep: now chilled with fear, aching to turn back, and now enthralled with desire, pressing forward until the water laps his feet. What long-submerged secrets await here? He has seen the throb of the iris, the winter sky's violence; has known the olive tree's commiseration and the stars' libations. But this—
Slowly he wades knee-deep into the blue-black lake. Far beneath
him, past the quivering line of a sudden drop, is the glimmer of   unknown things: not the baubles of some broken treasure-ship, but relics, older and stranger than what man has made, each a sacrament enrobed in waves. Their shapes ripple and blink, toying with Vincent's gaze, refusing definition; but he is certain of his mission. He will have them. He must have them. He forgets that his limbs are untested in such waters; he does not consider the power of the undertow, the piercing pain of stolen air. He stretches out his arms to swim, poises to propel himself there, down there—

Voices startle him into stepping back. There is a faceless crowd gathered on the shore, on higher ground, and they call out to him as one to come back, it is not safe, he will die . . .

"I have to go in," Vincent cries, but he can hear the terror in their reply. "There are better ways," they beseech. "Down the beach—you will find a store. Everything in the deep, is also there; but it is clean, and you need not drown for your prize. Please, take our advice—"

Vincent squints. He is at first disbelieving, but in the distance is the outline of a thatched little building, its roof catching up the remaining sun through a gap in the clouds. How peaceful it looks, even from here. There is a murmur of approval as he returns to the sand and starts toward the store. It seems it will be years before he reaches its door, but the miles dwindle to mere steps, so that it is only seconds before he has passed through the straw frame into the dry space within.

The attendant is grizzled and bent, his white hair falling to his shoulders. He sits behind a high counter and eyes Vincent without a word. The register at his hand is dustless, strangely current in contrast with both its keeper and the hut's crude walls, but in a moment, Vincent has forgotten this. He wanders through the shelves agape with wonder at what mer- chandise rests there, each piece tagged with its price and sparkling in the artificial light.

He cannot give a name to a single article, though there is a faint gleam of familiarity in each, brief and heartening like an old cadence woven into a foreign song. Words and memories, sensations and histories, flutter birdlike in him and then explode into flight, soaring beyond his reach. He touches a surface here, a texture there, and each time pulls back, shocked by its verve. To steady his nerves he wraps his arms around his waist, only to find a canvas bag belted there, laden with silver. He is at first bewil- dered— then voracious. Heady with the understanding that he can have whatever he wishes, he rushes to a table in a corner and lifts his trophy from its surface.

It is a seashell, but not. Massive, intricate, labyrinthine, it spirals outward only to loop back upon itself in an impossible design. In its opalescent skin Vincent finds sable and rose and the coral of the blushing sky. And there are hieroglyphs, missives from another world, etched into the curves like the figuring of a burl. When Vincent holds it to his ear, there is a waterfall's din, and then, he has a vision: a lone man paddling downriver, toward a frothing drop he cannot possibly survive . . .

"Is that what you wish to buy?" the grizzled man asks.

Vincent jumps. "Yes." He approaches the high counter with his prize in his arms. Oh, what he will do with this, and how deliciously easy it had been to attain! A simple lifting from a table—an exchange of coins— against the agony of long afternoons in the field, the torture of sleepless nights! Why had he wasted so much time? And to think he had come so close to the deep dive, the plunge into the black where he might have lost his life—

He is triumphant, almost smug. He is about to reach for the silver in his bag, when the shell trembles of its own accord. Then horror: a black, slithering creature, many-eyed with glinting teeth and long claws, darts out of the shell's belly toward Vincent as if its sole object is to consume him.

Vincent screams. He drops the shell and the hideous creature slinks away, glancing back at him with a simpering smile before it vanishes down a hole.

The old man is unsurprised. "Guess the shell wasn't yours to have," he says simply. Then he points out the door. "The sun is coming down. You don't have much time."

Nauseous and shaking, Vincent exits the store. He hikes back up the shore—the distance is real now, the trek long and taxing—toward his beginning. At last he reaches the place where the dream first led him. The crowd resorts to begging him, protesting his choice as he passes them by. They remind him of the danger, ask him why, why . . . He turns to tell them about the shell, then stops, realizing they don't want to know. He faces the water alone. He fixes one foot on the pebbled shore, feeling the stones dig into his soles as he anchors himself there. Then, still shaking, he lowers the other foot into the depths, and reaches down.

The sun is gone but it does not slumber. Somewhere beyond Vincent's vision it falls into contradiction, sweeping its lighthouse beam across its own story in the wake of munificent glory. Vincent reaches lower still. His fingertips brush something that cannot be bought, something for which wars must be fought. This is the lesson; this is the way. If only he could remember it by day . . . He can feel himself waking. In fear of forgetting, he builds a prayer like a bridge between the sea that he dreams and the land that he is. *Oh God, let me be a fertile field, so that each time You pass through, whatever falls from Your pockets will take root.*

Elizabeth Genovise's fiction has appeared in several dozen journals and has won numerous awards including the O. Henry Prize. She is the author of five collections of short stories, the most recent being *Lighthouse Dreams* from Passengers Press. Her first novel, *Third Class Relics*, is due out from Texas Review Press in 2024. Currently she teaches literature and creative writing to her community in east Tennessee.

THOMAS ALLBAUGH

A Table Story

After they took away the chairs and the table with the permanent food stains and scratch marks where their son always ate, he remained in the empty dining room thinking about it. You could always replace the furniture. But not the marks. You could buy distressed jeans but not distressed furniture, unless it was someone else's at Goodwill. Then it was someone else's history, family.

Most of the house felt empty. He brought a folding chair in from the hallway where the open cabinet was empty of towels, opened the folding chair in the middle of the floor, and sat down. He rubbed his elbow. His collar bone had healed; he still had some pain in the morning when the air was cold. After about six months, it was mostly just aching in his shoulder.

The call that she was coming for the table had left him out of sorts and he hadn't slept. He wasn't sure if she would come when they took the furniture. And then she didn't come. He glanced at the window. Perhaps he would use a tray table now.

She had not taken their bed, with the memory foam mattress that held their wounds night after night.

He rubbed his eyes. The folding chair wasn't comfortable. They were made for auditoriums

*

He went for a walk. After a few blocks, he came to a field left wild in the summer and fenced in, the now dry weeds a brittle dead wildness kept from the rest of the neighborhood, an abandoned garden of Eden, with chain-link fences instead of angels with swords of fire. He looked at the weeds nodding there and thought about the memorial service. Her family had mostly stayed away. Those who came ignored him. Word had spread quickly, of course, and opinions were certain. He glanced at the clouds beyond the trees and houses on the other side of the field and then back

at the wild field where the weeds went up to the fence. The thought came to him. "Only You bring good from evil." Though he had not stopped looking at the weeds, he realized that what he'd said was directed to God. He glanced up instinctively, said, "I wait for you to do this. How does this work, good from evil? I can't picture it. I can't do it."

He was beyond caring that he had never done this before, except maybe in childhood. He had never made a vow as an adult. Well, he had at their wedding, but that was different. That was two people, planning, agreeing, no matter what, about something that people did all the time and succeeded at.

This new one he didn't know how to live with, because he didn't know and couldn't know. The freeway incident had happened so fast and it was over and they still had no suspect. All he had done was cut someone off, sort of accidentally.

It was the "sort of" part that left him sad. In the church he and his wife had attended, people would often make vows. But then what happened? He'd never seen how they worked out. One of the last times he went—after his wife had stopped going with him—one of the ladies who still talked to him had said, "Just think how God suffered the loss of His son." This was meant to be profound about suffering and the problem of evil. It was supposed to make him think. But he was so sad about the "sort of" part and how he was to blame, and then he got lost in the labyrinth of theology the comparison naturally opened up on. He thought about his part in it.

*

In the evening, he sat under the patio light in the back yard. He couldn't see the neighboring yards, with the walls that surrounded his own.

Suddenly, to his left, the neighbor's garage light went on and then the neighbor came out, a tall man, his full head of black hair and a black mustache.

The neighbor waved. He set the trash he had brought out down and walked through the gate and came over to him. "So your wife left," the neighbor said.

He nodded.

"Road rage," the neighbor said, "what can you do? I mean them, not you."

He stared at the dark shape of the grill, nodded absently.

After a moment, the neighbor said, "Well, if you need anything, let me know."

"Thanks." He glanced at his neighbor's mustache. It was black. Did he use hair coloring?

He had not seen it this close before. He said, "You know, some people don't become better than themselves until they have children."

The neighbor stared at him. He was big enough to be a bouncer at a club. "I didn't start trying," he said, almost to something he'd been thinking about rather than what had been said, "until the birth of my son. That's what it took." He re-crossed his legs.

His neighbor bowed his head. "I really can't imagine what you are going through." He glanced into the dark. "But if you need something, let us know." He turned and went back to his yard, picked up the trash bags, and disappeared.

He watched him walk away. He was tall.

Before she had left, his wife had on several occasions heard sounds

49

coming from their yard by the neighbor's house, usually in the daytime. She had thought that their son's friends had come back to play in there. But every time she sent him out to look, the RV space was empty, quiet. The bikes not used or moved from where they had been left leaning against the fence. No one was there.

Next door, a door closed. He watched the neighbor's garage lights go out.

Thomas Allbaugh's poems and stories have appeared in a variety of journals, including *Modern Poetry Quarterly Review*, *Relief*, and *River Heron Review*. He's published a novel, *Apocalypse TV*, a collection of short stories, *Subtle Man Loses His Day Job* and other stories, and a chapbook of poetry titled *The View* from January. He is a professor of English at Azusa Pacific University, where he teaches composition and creative writing.

SETH WIECK

Under The Sun

Tommy scanned the horizon toward the Lees' house but saw no signs of his cousin Maggie. He jumped from the tractor steps as wind gusted through the crop along the north fence line, sifting toward him. Heat reflected off the yellow wheat and swung the air up and around itself into a dust devil that sucked chaff and fallen stalks into the sky. The devil swirled around him in the road and finally dropped the chaff into the thin stand of wheat behind him. The grain had withered in the drought and this field didn't produce enough to harvest, so his uncle Lee-boy hired him to plow it under. Tommy's stomach growled.

Dust finally billowed along the county road and sunlight glinted off a windshield. The brown Ford pickup he was expecting fishtailed around the corner, barreling down the road with a wake of dust spreading out over the crop. The tires bounced along the road, and his cousin Maggie peered through the steering wheel. She slid to a stop next to the tractor. A whisper of dust silted on the beards of wheat. Maggie waited inside the cab until the dirt settled and then jumped out carrying a lunchbox and a thermos.

"Sorry I'm late. Mom went to the café to get sweet tea."

"Tell Lee-girl thanks." Tommy looked at the tractor and back to Maggie. "I'm hungry."

They rested in the shade of the tractor, and Maggie unpacked meatloaf sandwiches on thick heels of wheat bread, wrapped in paper towels. She wore her blonde hair long and down. Stray curls would fall in her face until her eyes were hidden, and then she'd flick the curls aside to look him in the eye. It caught him by surprise every time.

"This is good," he said, lifting his sandwich.

"Glad you like it." She leaned back on one hand. "You're gonna have a birthday tomorrow."

"*We're* gonna have a birthday."

"Do you think God meant something, making us born on the same day?"

"It means our moms had sex with our dads about the same time." She rolled her eyes. He sighed, changing his tone.

"I'm an accident. All these grown ups around and no one knows who my dad is. Then they tell me that you can't have kids unless you're married, but nobody was married that had me. Couldn't have been too much meant by it."

"You ever try to figure out who your dad is?"

"In the mirror. I see my mom and some of your dad, but they're twins. I'm bound to have whatever he's made of in me."

"You look different. You must be growing."

"Not as fast as the boys in town. They all got armpit hair."

"Gross."

"It's just what it is."

She leaned back, the sun on her face, and her hair dropped back between her shoulders and touched the ground.

He opened the thermos and tilted it to his mouth, a trickle running over his lips and rinsing a line through the dust that had settled on his face. He wiped the wet away. Maggie held him steadily in her gaze.

"I think God meant something by it," she said. "I'll always be attached to you."

"If we're meant to be attached, then I guess I'll look after you."

"Do I need looking after?" she asked.

"I don't know that answer. I gotta get back to work." He stood and climbed the steps. "Thanks for the tea."

The tractor started with puffs of blue smoke, and he pushed the throttle forward and dropped the machine into gear. He twisted in the seat to watch Maggie, but she was already halfway down the road dragging a train of dust behind her.

That night it rained. Not a lot but enough that the roads would be mucked up. During the storm, Tommy woke from a dream. He lay on the bed looking into the dark and seeing nothing. "Hello?" he said.

He got up and crossed the hall to Maggie's room. "Maggie," he whispered.

She didn't stir.

He walked down the hall to his aunt and uncle's bedroom.

"Lee."

"Hmm?" she answered out of the dark. His Uncle Lee-boy snored quietly.

"Did you call me?" Tommy said.

"No."

Tommy walked back to his room and got in bed. Heaviness pulled at him and he sank back to sleep.

Again he woke in the darkness, his heartbeat quickened, his breath shallow so as not to miss what he thought he heard.

He got out of bed and crossed the hall to Maggie's room. He listened to her breathing in the dark and then went to his aunt and uncle again.

"Lee."

"Yes?" Lee-girl said.

"Did you call me?"

"No. Go back to bed."

He lingered in the doorway listening for any sounds in the house. The clock in the kitchen ticked. He held his breath, listening to the second hand moving, and then his body urged him to breathe again. He walked to his bedroom and got under the covers. He exhaled and rested. His fingers tingled and his flesh grew tired. He slept again.

He swam to the surface at the sound of his name for the third time. He threw back the covers and ran to the Lees'. He knelt on Lee-girl's side of the bed.

"Lee."

"What?"

"Did you call me?"

Lee-boy sat up. "Who's there?"

"It's Tommy," she said. "It's okay."

Lee-boy dropped to his pillow and mumbled.

"Tommy," she said, "what did it sound like?"

"Someone called my name."

She sighed. "I want you to go back to bed, and if you hear it again just say, 'Here I am.' Maybe it's the Lord." She rubbed her eyes. "Can you do that?"

"Yes."

"All right. Go back to bed."

He lay on his back, blinking in the dark as the rain tapped on his window. He heard it again. In a motion he was out of bed, yanking the closet light on, and then back in bed to hide under the covers from the voice that called his name.

In the morning he opened his eyes to Lee-girl lying next to him. She'd been watching him.

"What happened?" she said. "Tell me everything."

"It was just a dream."

"Thomas Moor, tell me what happened."

"I was scared so I turned the light on." He looked over Lee-girl's head into the closet.

"Why'd you get scared? The Lord isn't gonna hurt you."

"How do you know it was God, Lee-girl? I coulda been hearing things."

"You could be hearing God," she said. "What most people would give for that."

"I turned the light on. I think most people would have done the same."

"I wouldn't have." She rolled out of bed.

"Then God should have called you instead. He ruined my

sleep!"

Rubbing his eyes, he followed her into the kitchen. Maggie was scrambling eggs. "Happy birthday," she said.

"You too." he said. "Thirteen. We aint kids no more."

Maggie scooped eggs onto four plates, and Lee-girl put bread in the toaster and sliced apples. Lee-boy came in and twitched a smile and a nod in Tommy's direction, and poured a cup of coffee. The pot clanked in the machine.

Tommy said, "Can you grab me a cup while you're there?"

Lee-girl looked up from the apples. "When did you start drinking coffee?"

"As soon as he gets over here with that cup, I guess." He took only two sips the whole meal. The first one burned his tongue.

Lee-boy drove him to the tractor after breakfast. Tommy gazed out the rolled-down window. Nine o'clock and ninety degrees. Heat shimmers blurred the horizon all the way around.

"You think the fields are dry enough?" asked Tommy.

"Yep."

"Can you cut today?"

"The west place should be ready this afternoon."

"You want me to help?"

"After you finish sweeping this field. If you're done before lunch, come back in with Maggie. I'll pick you up at the house."

The rain had washed the dust off the tractor windshield. The remaining acres to be plowed appeared clearly. Tommy reached for the choke and the key and cranked the engine. He set the throttle, dropped the tractor into gear, and cut a new line in the crust where the mud had dried. Under the crust the dirt was dark and moist. Tommy kept the windows open, letting the wind drag off some of the heat. After three rounds he could see his earlier work changing color and drying in the heat, and then the dust began to rise from the plow. He closed the windows on eastbound rounds because the westerly wind that was steadily rising pushed the dust and enveloped the tractor. With the windows closed, the tractor cab became an oven, so he shed his T-shirt. Sweat shone on his skin and then chalked with the dirt filtering through the faulty window seals.

The tractor pulled a fourteen-foot plow, and a full round took twenty minutes, eating away the morning, three rounds an hour.

On a westbound round, he opened the thermos and poured the water into his mouth. The overflow ran down his chest and cut a swath through the dust. The cool refreshed him. He shut the thermos and set it back in the wedge between the seat and the wheel well.

Along the edge of the field, a coyote loped. "You're brave out in the daylight," he said.

The coyote crouched into the wheat. Signs of its path appeared. Then a big-eared jackrabbit burst out, the coyote bounding after it. The rabbit easily outstripped the coyote until a second coyote, posted ahead of the rabbit, lunged out of the wheat and caught the jackrabbit by the back of the neck. The first coyote trotted up, and the two of them shared the meal.

Nine rounds and it was noon. Ten rounds and it was almost half-past. His stomach growled with hunger.

"Where are you, Maggie?"

Twelve rounds and he was nearly done with what was left of the field, but he was hungry. He pulled the rig over to the road running through the property and sat with the engine idling for a while, watching for the cloud of dust on the county road that meant she was coming. Nothing. He turned the key and pulled the kill switch, and the engine wheezed to a stop. He grabbed the thermos and his shirt and stepped off the tractor.

His stomach growled as he walked east toward the Lees'. He looked back to the field.

"Just finish," he said, but his stomach urged him on and he kept walking. In a mound of dirt he saw a padded paw print that had broken through the crust. "There's the coyote, rabbit. Coming to get you. You don't even know he exists, but he's on his way."

He kicked the dirt mound and the paw print scattered over the gray crust. The air sponged the heat and carried more than its own weight down his lungs. He walked north now, toward the county road. "Where you at, Maggie?"

When he turned the corner toward the Lees' he saw the brown pickup, wheels up, in the ditch. He ran. Just before he reached it he stumbled through a deep rut and fell into the weeds beside the truck. The driver's side lay facing the ditch, and the soft dirt had been dug away. He crawled to the driver's door.

"Maggie, you here?" The back window was busted out and tiny bits of glass sparkled in the dirt. A trail in the dirt and crushed wheat stalks led away from the truck, then doubled back toward the ditch. An imprint of Maggie's body lay in the dried crust of dirt, and blood, then dragging footsteps away from the wreck. He ran along the road, passing her shirt drenched in blood, and came upon her lying in the ditch in her bra and shorts.

The left side of her face was black with the blood and dirt and her eye was smashed shut, her nose turned. Mud caked her mouth and hair. Her left leg twisted above the knee.

He moved to lift her but stopped to judge the distance to the Lees'.

A mile, at least.

"I'm going get your dad."

He ran, stumbling through ruts. His mouth dried as he ran and there was no air. He ran and his legs hurt and his feet were hot, rubbing in his boots, his toes jamming in the boots he'd outgrown. He walked until his breath came back to him and he ran again. When he burst in through the back door, his aunt and uncle could see there was something wrong and grabbed the truck keys before he explained. In the truck, he finally was able to coax some words from his parched mouth, but all he could say was that Maggie was hurt.

At the wreck, they loaded Maggie into the pickup and roared down the road, leaving Tommy by the ditch. He watched them and their dust go, and then he walked through the wheat toward the tractor.

"Finish the field." When he came to the road that ran through the field, he crumpled like a hollow reed next to the wheat under the sun. He lay in the dirt, the beards of skimpy wheat no shelter from the scorching sun, his pupils shrinking against the light.

"Here I am," Tommy said. "Here I am."

Seth Wieck's stories, essays, and poetry can be read in *Narrative Magazine*, *Ekstasis*, *Grand Little Things*, and *The Broad River Review* where he won the Ron Rash Award in Fiction. He's currently a candidate for an MFA at the University of St. Thomas in Houston, and lives in Amarillo with his wife and three children.

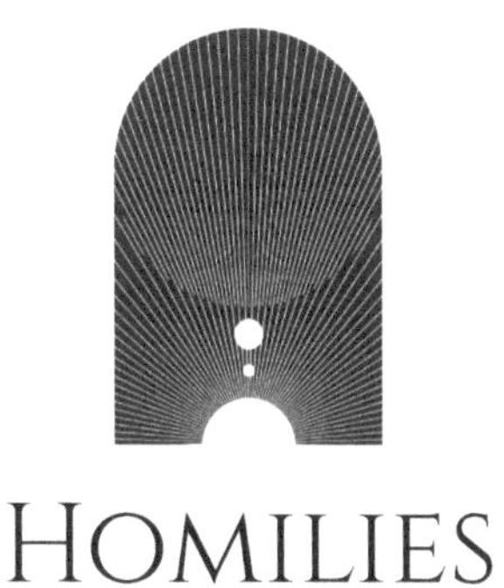

HOMILIES

E. J. Boston

Remembrance – A Homily on Luke 23

We have forgotten God's faithfulness and we have forgotten our faithlessness, but Jesus takes our forgetfulness and promises to remember us faithfully.

Though we forget, we are not forgotten.

The Problem of Memory
Memory is a problem. The older we get, the more often we walk from one room to another only to have forgotten what brought us there in the first place. The humor of age and memory fades quickly for those who have loved ones who suffer more severely.

If you've ever known someone with dementia or Alzheimer's, you know the pain of forgetfulness. Names and memories begin to slip away and personality traits that were hidden beneath the surface become more prominent. The strange behaviors of the ones we love become a source of pain, and we begin to wonder if they're even the same person. Much of our relationships depend upon shared memory, things that we can recall. Is your parent really your parent if they can't remember you as their child? Memory loss affects us as a result of the fall, but it was not intended to be our common experience.

The intent of a delightful land (Genesis 1-2)
When God created us, he created us as his image-bearers: those who would represent him to the world. We were intended to enact his character and presence for the whole world. We were a monument of God . . . one might even say that we were supposed to remember him for the

benefit of all. We were intended to dwell in the delightful land of God's presence. A place where memory was not something distant, but something actual—the same way that spouses 'remember' their wedding vows by daily practicing acts of love. We were intended to inhabit the garden paradise and to expand God's creative love to the end of all creation.

The accusations against God (Malachi 3)
And yet despite the invitation to live in constant memory of God's beauty and love, our first parents chose to forget God's words. "Did God really say?" the serpent asked. And though we knew what God had really said, we chose to forget the promise and to believe a lie. We chose to inhabit the

world of the serpent instead of the world of God. We chose to disown and forget God's goodness instead of relishing in it.

Malachi 3 shows us how far we have gone to forget God's goodness. "How have we wearied God?" we ask like a child looking for excuses. "By saying that we have worshiped him in vain." How often we look to things we have done and believe that God has been unjust in our portion. "Look at everything I have done," we want to say, "and God has not repaid me as is my due!" We speak as though we could persuade God's action. And we forget not only God's goodness throughout our life, but we forget our own sinfulness. We forget God's faithfulness and we forget our own faithlessness.

The Book of Remembrance (Revelation 13:8)
But God has not forgotten us. Like Adam and Eve we forget that he has given us every tree of the garden, and we forget that we have left him for the lie of the snake. Like the priests in Malachi's prophecy, we forget that God has promised to dwell with his people through their faithfulness, and we forget that we have illegitimately demanded God respond to our timeline and practices. Like our beloved companions that suffer from memory loss, we have forgotten the things that have mattered most, and we have become like different people.

But God has not forgotten us. Though we forget, we are not forgotten.

God promised his people through the prophet Malachi that he would prepare a book of his people. He would write down their name and gather them as his inheritance. He would inscribe our name like a king writes down the deeds of victories won and children's inheritances. In that day, the Day of the Lord, when fire purifies the earth, he will save his precious treasure; they will not be forgotten. But how can this be? How can God remember us despite our failing? How can God inscribe our name when it is tainted by bloodguilt and mire?

Though our names are tainted with forgetfulness, forgetting his faithfulness and forgetting our faithlessness, he made a promise. And God does not forget his promises.

God took to himself human flesh and lived among us. He did not forget the word of God, but lived the word of God. In perfect memory of the Father's faithfulness, he denied the words of the serpent and remembered God's word. He remembered the Father's faithfulness to care for the least of these. He was repaid with persecution and betrayal, but in the Garden, he did not forget the Father's faithfulness.

And after living in perfect memory of the Father, he took our forgetful, human flesh and he marched it to the forsaken tree that we who were faithless might not be forgotten.

The Path to Paradise
Luke 23 depicts Jesus, the Son, having been tried and sentenced. He has been given the wooden beam, and foreigners have marched alongside him. But there are others there too. There are women there, following him and weeping (Lk. 23:27ff.).

The words of Jesus are shocking and offensive. As he turns to the women following and weeping, he tells them, "Do not weep for me. Instead weep for yourselves and your children." The day is coming, he tells them, when the tree will be dry, perhaps referring to the day of judgment, when people will beg the mountains and hills to crush and cover them, to hide them from the judgment coming upon the earth. "Do not weep for me, but weep for yourselves." In so doing, Jesus reminds us that he goes willingly because he follows the word of the Father in the power of the Spirit.

And going along with him were two others. Others of a different kind. These were evildoers, and though Jesus was sentenced, they could hardly be considered similar. The ones who went alongside him were not righteous or faithful. They were unrighteous and faithless. These are the ones who rebel against God and man and are receiving their just punishment.

And when they reach the place of the skull they crucify him. It is remarkable that Luke's depiction is bloodless. This is a crucifixion, there is no doubt, but the text only uses one matter-of-fact way of stating it: "There they crucified him." There is no spear in the side, there is no crown of thorns, there is no whip, and there is no blood. The pure and spotless lamb of God is maligned and mocked, but the cross is his throne. Outside of the city, in the wilderness country, the blameless lamb was laden down with curses (Lev. 16:21). Jesus surely is the Passover lamb, and he surely is the burnt bull; but here in Luke 23, Jesus is the Azazel Goat. He is not depicted as the slaughtered one. He is shown as the pure one who bears away the sins of the people; damns them in the desert, sinks them in the sea. God has no problem with memory: he forgets only what he chooses to, and he chooses to forget our sin.

Though all others seemed to forget his righteousness, he did not forget why he had come to the earth.

"Father, forgive them, for they do not know what they do."

He came as a perfect priest to intercede for the people and bring purification. He came as the spotless lamb to receive the confession and transgression of the people and to take it far into the wilderness. As the Scapegoat, Jesus came to bear away the sin . . . even the sin that the people *do not know what they do.*

Did you know that God made provision for sins of ignorance? There are things we have forgotten we had done, but God provided a way for Israel to trust that God has absolved forgotten sin. When Jesus climbs upon the cross, with evildoers on his left and his right, he stretches out his hands and says, "Father, forgive them, for they do not know what they do."

They have forgotten! They do not even know the things they have done. They do not even know the things they have not done. They do not even know the things God has done that they have failed to notice. For all the forgotten sins, Jesus prays, "Forgive them." It is vain to serve God, we think, because he has forgotten us and he has let the wicked escape; but

God remembers us even when we forget.

Those standing there watched while Jesus was the purifying priest, praying for all around him. The encampment watched. As the perfect lamb, he received their transgressions.

The rulers cast lots and called him the chosen one at the same time that they scoffed: "Let him save himself!"

Oh, but Jesus is the chosen one, the anointed priest who would serve the people.

The soldiers brought wine and called him the King of the Jews at the same time that they mocked him: "Save yourself!"

Oh, but Jesus *is* the King of the Jews, exalted upon the cross, his throne, and there is even the inscription written above him, telling the whole world that *he is the king.*

The evildoer called upon Christ for salvation at the same time as he blasphemed him: "Save yourself and us!"

Oh, but Jesus *is* saving them, though he himself did not need salvation. He is the savior of all who look to him.

But the other evildoer knew Jesus' righteousness. Through the Holy Spirit's light shining into his heart, he saw the faithfulness of Jesus. So he asked... not that he would remember Jesus, but that Jesus would remember him. He honored him as the Covenant Keeper when he asked, "Remember me." The other one blasphemed Jesus, but not both. One of them saw Jesus and asked why he was doing nothing to save them. But the other rebuked him and remembered the just judgment of God. He remembered the faithfulness of the Covenant Keeper. He remembered the faithlessness of his own transgressions. And instead of asking Jesus to prove himself, he trusted him to be everything. "Remember me," he asked, and the goat that would bear the sin into the place of forgetfulness promised that he would remember him indeed.

"Truly, I say to you, today you will be with me in paradise."

Jesus promised to remember him, but not as a distant, historical fact. As a spouse can remember their wedding day, Jesus remembers us always. Paradise, a return to the garden, is something that is future in scope, but it is not only future just as it is not only past. It is something that takes place every day and every week. Though we forget, we are not forgotten.

Jesus carried our sin to the wilderness to be forever forgotten, but he promises to remember us always. And he does so through his Holy Spirit. His Spirit dwells with us and brings to us the favor of the Father. The Holy Spirit brings us into the living memory of God's faithfulness. He causes us to remember God's goodness, and he teaches us what is in the Lamb's Book of Life.

Forgetting is painful. But it is most painful when we forget the things we ought to remember and remember the things we ought to forget.

Do not fear . . . for even when we forget, we are not forgotten.

E. J. Boston is an Applied Theology graduate of California Baptist University and an M.Div candidate at Beeson Divinity School (Birmingham, AL). He regularly fills the pulpit of churches in need, and explores storytelling through narrative role-playing games. His beautiful wife Ruthie has been a faithful encouragement, and his two sons remind him of the need to proclaim God's grace and truth to all humanity. Though he has delivered conference papers in theology and written informally, he is glad to have Solum become the home of his first published work.

PAUL J. PASTOR

The Narrow Door

A Homily for August 21, 2022, preached at All Souls Anglican Church, in Portland, Oregon.

Jesus went through one town and village after another, teaching as he made his way to Jerusalem. Someone asked him, 'Lord, will only a few be saved?' He said to them, 'Strive to enter through the narrow door; for many, I tell you, will try to enter and will not be able. When once the owner of the house has got up and shut the door, and you begin to stand outside and to knock at the door, saying, "Lord, open to us", then in reply he will say to you, "I do not know where you come from." Then you will begin to say, "We ate and drank with you, and you taught in our streets." But he will say, "I do not know where you come from; go away from me, all you evildoers!" There will be weeping and gnashing of teeth when you see Abraham and Isaac and Jacob and all the prophets in the kingdom of God, and you yourselves thrown out. Then people will come from east and west, from north and south, and will eat in the kingdom of God. Indeed, some are last who will be first, and some are first who will be last.' Luke 13: 22-30 NRSV

May the words of my mouth and the meditation of my heart be pleasing in your sight, O Lord, my Rock and my Redeemer. Amen.

***

Today, I would like us to meditate upon the difficult and misunder- stood concept of *narrowness*. This is the theme that, if you look for it unites all the Church's traditional readings today, finding its most clear expression in the passage that we just received–Christ's teaching of The Narrow Door.

There is perhaps no other doctrine so poised to prompt a reaction from contemporary people, especially Portlanders such as ourselves. After all, barring the worst crimes, there is little seen worthy of judgment here besides judgmentalism. Little to be excluded besides attitudes of exclusivity. And though narrowness in the way Christ uses it does not neatly fall under the categories of either judgment nor exclusivity — at least not in the way we might define those terms, the moment we hear the word: "narrow" our minds, or at least the minds of our secular neighbors, are carried to the smallest, most cliched elements popularly associated with Christianity: the social archetypes of The Bigot or The Picketer with the "Turn or Burn" sign, or That Guy Who Leaves Evangelistic Tracts For Waitresses Instead of Tips.

I do not blame such a reflexive reaction, even if I believe it to be unfair. It is, at least in its beginnings, a *learned* reaction. Rather than the expansive grace, the unconditional love, and the sacrificial compassion that ought to mark the lives of Christ's followers, too often those associated with the name of Jesus have been small, judgmental, legalistic, rude, eager to condemn, and rather bad at parties. But of course, it is not the whole story, and even for us, the word "narrow" may need gentle reconsideration. In this, there is no better passage than our gospel reading this morning.

***

Our reading begins with a brief story, one which is found only in St. Luke's Gospel. Christ is making his way as an itinerant preacher through rural Judea, wending his way inevitably toward Jerusalem. And beside the ministry of miracles and healings which is spreading his fame through the country, it is his teaching in the classic style of the wandering rabbi that we glimpse here. On his way to Jerusalem, Jesus is asked a simple question by a member of the crowd: *Are only a few to be saved?* We quickly attach to this question. It is one we have asked as well. Besides the grand seminary hypotheticals — what of those who have never heard? — the question becomes poignant for us as there arise before us the faces of those we know, those perhaps whom we love, who we know with confidence are far from Christ, perhaps far by choice, by definite choice. *Are only a few to be saved?* Only those who say the magic prayer? Those born in the right time, and under favorable stars? Are only a few to be saved? Those lucky, those privileged?

And for us here, in 2022, in Portland, Oregon, we want Christ to respond to this question definitively and with a resounding *No!* We want him to answer with the full force of the Gospel message. That Good News so potently distilled by the apostle John, who wrote that God so loved the world that he gave his only begotten so, that whosoever — WHOSOEVER — believes in him might have everlasting life. We want him to quote St. Paul, who knew that God was reconciling all things — ALL THINGS — to the Father through Christ Jesus, Paul who further saw that Christ would be the firstborn of MANY brothers and sisters, not few, *MANY.*

We want to hear all this from Christ. But instead, we are given a mysterious cluster of cryptic phrases. And among those phrases a single word stands tall, drawing all our eyes like the North Pole draws the compass needle: *"narrow."*

***

64

"Narrow." The Greek term translated here seems to be a very old word, older even than the proper Greek language itself. English gets it pretty much right: "narrow" is a good translation. "Tight" would be another. The old English translation of "strait" as in, say "the Straits of Magellan" is also pretty good. But it is the concept of danger and ability to fit that we ought to note here, and which ought to be our first clue that our common thinking about this word may not be faithful to the text. "Strive to enter through the narrow door," Jesus says, "for many, I tell you, will seek to enter and will not be *able*."

I think, when I read these words, of the longhouses of the Chinook peoples upon whose traditional lands we now are living. While many of their descendants remain here to this day, many tragedies, particularly post-contact disease, meant that entire tribes, bands, and clans, entire local dialects were lost within a matter of a few generations, mostly in the later 1700s and early 1800s. Because of our wet environment, and the Chinook tradition of building almost exclusively with wood, there is very little evidence of the density of population that was here before the settlement of European-descended people. But both oral tradition and our best archeological evidence indicate that here, in the Willamette Valley and extending up the Columbia Gorge was a rich and developed civilization, whose trade relationships extended from Alaska to far Southwest, from the Pacific Coast to deep in the continent's interior. Celilo Falls, now inundated deep under the waters of The Dalles Dam, was so bustling at the time of the salmon trading that it was called the "Wall Street of Native America," and it is said, likely reliably, that the greatest chief, whose name was Multnomah — whose name of course is living on among us in the names of many local places — could field an army of ten thousand young warriors clad in their famous "clamons" body armor, supple and nearly invulnerable, made from boiled elk hide.

I digress a bit. But humor me. Perhaps you have had the honor of going into a reconstruction of one of the Chinook longhouses, such as the Cathlapotle Plankhouse up in Ridgefield, Washington, reconstructed on the site of a village that dates at least to 1450. I have, and it is quite wonderful, making you feel at once the foolishness of the little personalized boxes that we shut ourselves up in in our culture. A longhouse belonged to an extended family, and depending on the size could house 40-80 people or more. The walls were made of great thick planks split from the rot-resistant, aromatic wood of the Western Red Cedar. The heart of the house was a sunken circular pit for a fire and cooking. The smoke from the pit went up toward a soaring ceiling high above the heads of the people. There were organized sections for raised food storage, for equipment storage, and areas, sometimes open, sometimes screened, for individual family units to have some semblance of personal space. Carved or painted figures told the ancestry and story of the family. Lavish feasting was of great value to the tribes, who excelled in preparing dishes of rich salmon and the cooked camas root, which had something like the flavor of a baked pear and the texture of a water chestnut. People of social status held what we call a potlatch in great honor, where the host would demonstrate their wealth and generosity with extravagant cuisine and hospitality and the giving of expensive gifts.

But of note is this fact: the plankhouse, this place of family and belonging, and feasting, and safety, and shelter, had no windows, and no doors, except for one. Can you call it a door? I am not sure you can. It is a hole. Sized perhaps three and a half or four feet. Positioned so that to get in, you must both duck your head and lift your feet to enter with a sort of awkward hop—quite uncomfortable, and allowing one or two people inside to quite effectively identify all entrants and, should it be needed, defend the house. I have seen the same principle in the walled city of York in England, and in the Gate of the ancient city of Megiddo in what is now Israel, and in cattle pens and the parts of old barns where you want to shear a sheep: narrowness. The pinch point. The moment of decision, of evaluation. Are you friend or enemy? Are you ready? Are you able to enter? *Are you known?* And like the plankhouse, such an eye is good.

***

Tight. Narrow. "Strive to enter through the narrow door," Jesus says, "for many, I tell you, will seek to enter and will not be able." And with that, just like that, we feel that Christ has said something he has not, something we fear is terrible, that calls into question the gospel being actually *good news* and so we miss what has actually been said.

And in this we are in danger of missing the key point of the whole exchange, because even though we think he has, *Christ did not answer the question.* Did you catch that? It was quick, with a rabbi's turn of cryptic phrase, quick in Christ's classic and disarming style. The question was simple and concrete: *Are only a few to be saved?* It demands a yes or a no. But what is said is neither of these, and is in fact a total *non sequitur*: "Strive to enter through the narrow door."

The importance of this cannot be overstated. Because we read the whole remainder of the passage as if it is the answer to this person's question: *when it is actually a subversion of that question, a redirection of that question to the point that really matters.* Christ turned what should have been exposition—here is the doctrine, my son—into *exhortation*: Get in. Prevail. Try to enter.

We are in the language of parable, here, of the image, of the teaching story. Not of doctrine. What is the clear teaching of this passage? An imperative. Get inside! Now! If you can fit, get in! We read the word *able* as *allowed*, in part because of our limited and judiciary understandings of salvation. But in that word, *able*, is a whole natural logic of the kingdom. The question is *can you fit?* This is not some ableist, fat-shaming question. It refers in no way to the body, but to a leanness, a thinness of soul. It puts us in mind of rich men like camels and the eyes of needles, or in mind of the Beatitude: *Blessed are the poor* (small, humble) *in spirit*, and we glimpse for a minute the fact that salvation is an extension of the logic of God seen present in all of Creation: what is able to live will live. What is incapable of life will die. To the one with much, more will be given, to the one who has not, even what he has will be taken away, and *oh* that sounds *so* unfair until you realize that Christ is teaching about *life*. The one with even a spark of it will be met like a child and welcomed home. The one who has become a servant of death will be, of course, unknown and unknowable to the Master of the feast of creation. It is not ours, is *never* ours to say who is who. That is the Master's job. It is ours to strive to enter to bend ourselves into the awkward bow of entrance. It is our job to try to join the feast.

What is the point? *Be known by the master of the house!* Don't wait. Don't stand out in the dark, when there is a feast going on inside. Oh, did you miss that? The feast? The one with the prophets and the patriarchs, and oh, I don't know, *People from the literal four corners of the earth?* Few to be saved? We are talking North and South and East and West reclining at table here. Boy, we should have liked Jesus to answer our question simply, but he has done something better. He has given us a vision of the eternal feast. And it is huge. Will few be saved? No. Many will not be able to fit, *but that is not the same thing as saying few will be saved.* The whole earth is there, all the misfits and rejects and sinners and beggars, and screw-ups and flops and *all* who can fit through the door, *all* who are known by the master of the feast and called to join the greatest party that the universe has ever known. But if you're "big"? You won't fit. Carrying the riches of your life with you? You won't fit. Trying to smuggle in your pet sin under your coat? Trying to bring your huge and polished righteousness? Try to name drop? "Oh yeah, I was with Jesus before it was cool." Sorry, you won't fit.

And is this not the holy and gentle harshness of the Good News? For there is light and there is darkness. There must be. It can be no other way. There are real stakes in the game, great stakes. There is inside and there is outside. There is first and there is last. There are those who are known and there are those who are not known. There is a *door*. Doors are made to open. They are also made to close. To deny this is to deny the heart of the Good News. But likewise, we deny the Good News when we allow anything

— anything — to distract from the broadness and welcome and simple generosity of the picture Christ paints for us here.

***

And so as we note that Christ has given us an icon, an *image* rather than cold doctrine, an image of a narrow door behind which sits a great feast, a banquet spread for the four corners of the earth by a careful and compassionate Master, as we hold this image in our mind today, to be faithful to the text we must allow Christ to challenge us: *are we willing to bow and be known, willing to enter through the narrow door to the great gift-giving, the mighty and unending feast?*

This looks, certainly, like the moment of salvation. But it also looks like the process of formation, what St. Paul calls "being saved." For as we come today to the table, and, much like stepping into a plankhouse, bend ourselves awkwardly and kneel, we are saying, *Know us Father. We are yours in Christ. His body for us, his blood for us. Let us keep the feast.* We are practicing here in time the central motion of eternity: the endless, all-consuming celebration.

Toward this, let us strive, undistracted by all lesser questions, always bending in Christlike humility to enter through that great and lovely paradox of the narrow door.

In the Name of the Father and the Son and the Holy Spirit, Amen.

Paul J. Pastor is an award-winning writer and editor (for HarperCollins), whose most recent book is *Bower Lodge: Poems*. His work has appeared widely, including in *The Los Angeles Review of Books, FORMA, The Windhover, Presence, Ekstasis, North American Anglican, Fathom,* and many other excellent outlets, and has been anthologized by the *New York Quarterly Review.* He lives in Oregon.

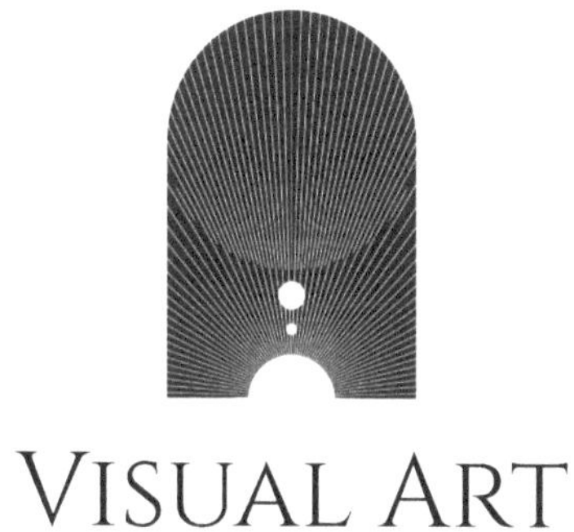

VISUAL ART

EDWARD LEE

Lee, *A Dream Reshapes*, 2022. Digital painting.

Lee, *Inertia*, 2022. Digital painting.

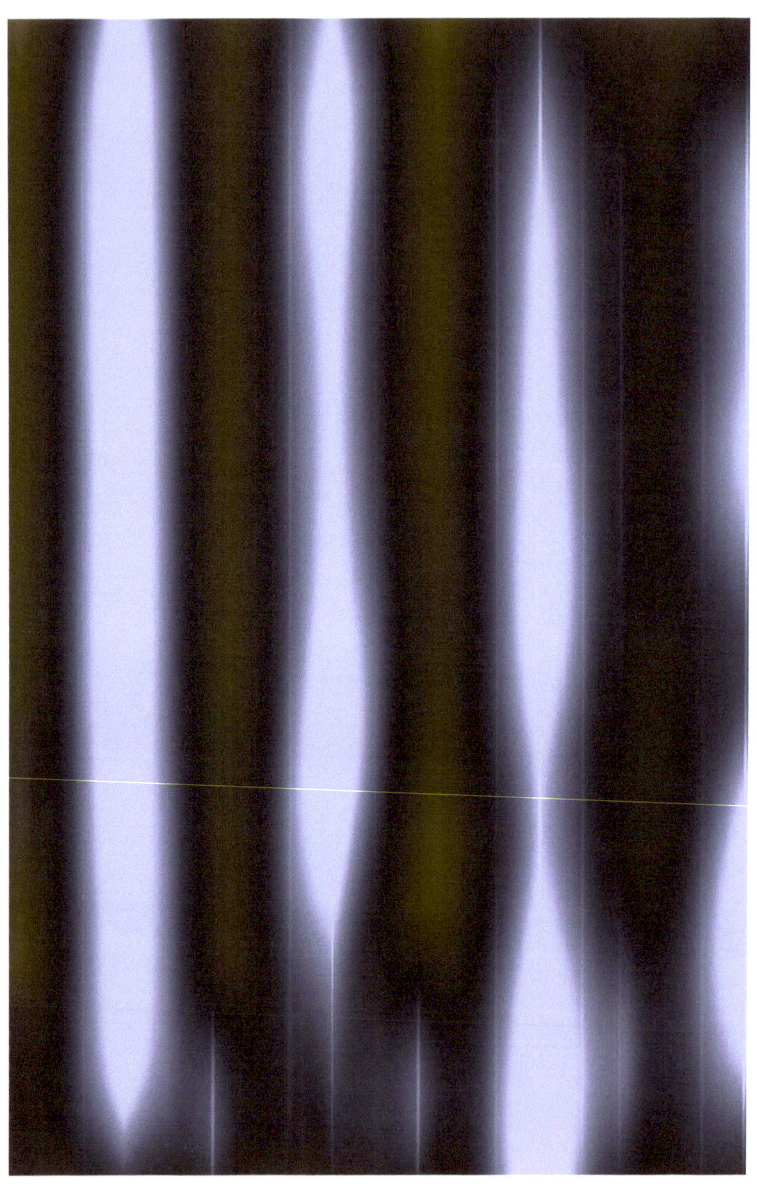

Lee, *Broken Blessings*, 2022. Digital painting.

Lee, *The Path to Reach*, 2022. Digital painting.

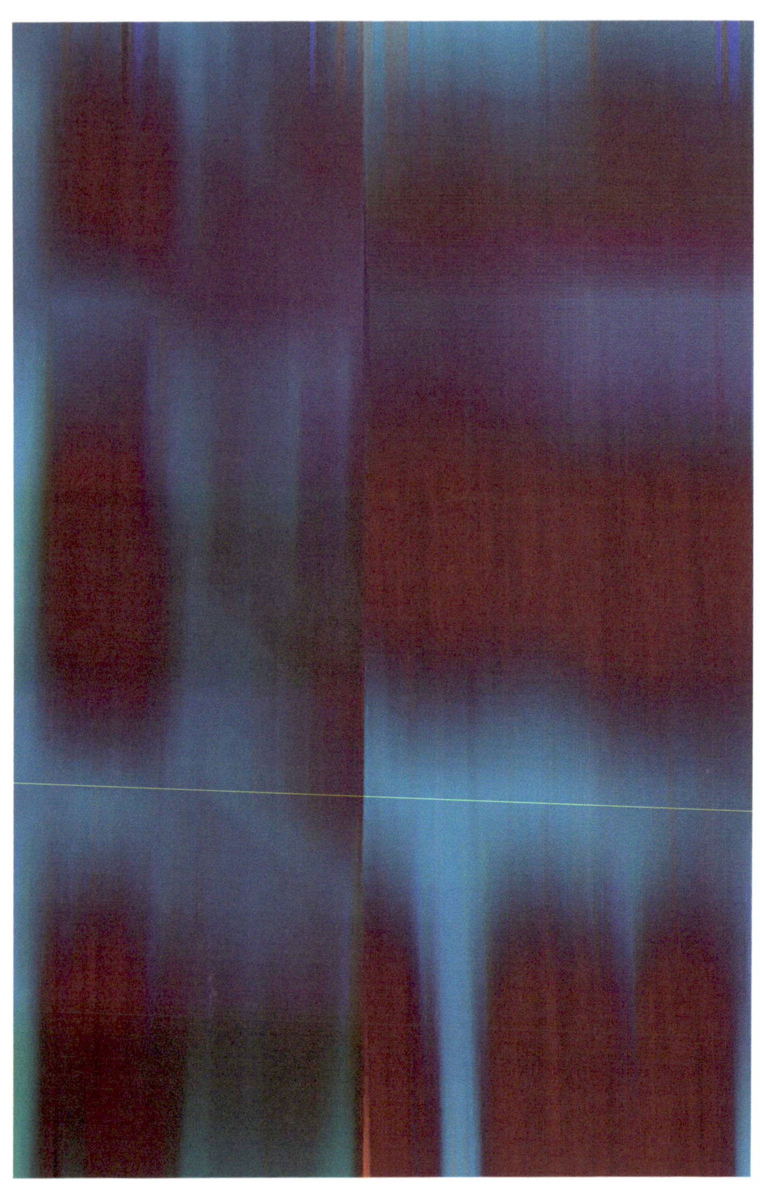

Lee, *Waterfall*, 2022. Digital painting.

Edward Lee is an artist and writer from Ireland. His paintings and photography have been exhibited widely, while his poetry, short stories, and non-fiction have been published in magazines in Ireland, England and America, including *The Stinging Fly*, *Skylight 47*, *Acumen* and *Smiths Knoll*. He is currently working on two photography collections: *Lying Down With The Dead* and *There Is A Beauty In Broken Things*.

He also makes musical noise under the names Ayahuasca Collective, Orson Carroll, Lego Figures Fighting, and Pale Blond Boy.

His blog/website can be found at https://edwardmlee.wordpress.com.